There are some who can live without wild things,
and some who cannot.

—*Aldo Leopold*

The
Sand Country
of
Aldo Leopold

A photographic interpretation by Charles Steinhacker
Essay by Susan Flader
Selections from the writings of Aldo Leopold
Edited, with an introduction, by Anthony Wolff
Designed by Charles Curtis

Sierra Club
San Francisco • New York

For Barbara, Little Katie, and all the young people who seek out nature's simple truths in order to find meaning in their own lives. —*C.S.*

For the family of Aldo Leopold. —*S.F.*

All photographs Copyright © 1973 by Charles Steinhacker. Used by permission.

The Leopold text was originally published in *A Sand County Almanac: and Sketches Here and There*. Copyright © 1949 by Oxford University Press.

Produced in New York by Charles Curtis and Lori Joseph. Filmset in 12 point Times Roman by TypoGraphic Innovations, Inc., New York. Printed and bound in Italy by Mondadori Editore, Verona. Library of Congress Catalogue Card No. 73-85045. International Standard Book No. ISBN 87156—075—5.

The Sierra Club, founded in 1892 by John Muir, has devoted itself to the study and protection of the nation's scenic and ecological resources—mountains, wetlands, woodlands, wild shores and rivers, deserts and plains. All club publications are part of the nonprofit effort the club carries on as a public trust. There are more than 40 chapters coast to coast, in Canada, Hawaii and Alaska. Participation is invited in the Club's program to enjoy and preserve wilderness and the quality of life everywhere. For membership information and other data on how you can help, please address inquiries to: Sierra Club, Box S.C.L., 1050 Mills Tower, San Francisco, California 94104.

Introduction

Aldo Leopold first came to the sand counties of central Wisconsin on a hunting trip in 1925. A decade later he bought a derelict farm there, and he died nearby in 1948, shortly after consigning his sand county essays to publication. The few years of weekends and occasional longer retreats at his sand county shack, transmuted into *A Sand County Almanac,* were as intimate a collaboration between a man and a landscape as has ever existed in life or in literature.

Leopold brought to his used-up, backwater homestead a lifelong love of the natural world, intensified by a sensitive appreciation of the mechanisms that made the living system succeed. In that small, impoverished universe, his appreciation took root in precise observation, and his love flowered into poetry; and poetry and observation merged in *A Sand County Almanac* that is neither art nor science, but both inseparable. It was as though the very modesty of the sand counties—the gift of geologic history and human stewardship—abetted the climactic effort of Leopold's life. The simplified landscape became an open

Aldo Leopold

ecological text to the perceptive student, and an analogue to the spare lucidity of his prose.

With Aldo Leopold's brief, productive tenancy, the isolated sand counties became the junction of two main currents in the conservation mainstream. One was the undying aesthetic-religious nature-passion of the 19th century Romantics and Transcendentalists: Muir, Thoreau, *et al.* The other was the methodical, dispassionate ecological research of emergent science. Leopold's life and work brought the two together in a synthesis for all seasons, most especially for our own. His "land ethic" applied scientific reason to human values, without recourse to external authority, raising a secular, ecological standard to which even we of little faith can repair, and by which we can survive. *A Sand County Almanac,* Leopold's gentle manifesto, mediates the schism between science and humanism that has been diagnosed as symptomatic of our century. The modest volume's spontaneous popularity, which continues to increase more than two decades after its unheralded debut, testifies to the persuasive force of Leopold's insight.

Those who have come through Leopold's work to share his lucid appreciation of life's essential elegance will find the style of this volume faithful to its inspiration. For those who have heretofore had to infer Leopold's landscape from his prose, the photographs of Charles Steinhacker, who conceived the idea for this book, offer a unique opportunity to see the context from which Leopold's words take their original impetus and meaning. Susan Flader, devoted archivist and student of Leopold's life and work, describes his sand county experience in the larger setting of the area's history and Leopold's own life.

And from Aldo Leopold himself, this volume includes a quintessential selection from *A Sand County Almanac: and Sketches Here and There.* The quotations serve not only as a primer of Leopold's work, but also as distilled evidence of the persistent timeliness of his ideas and the imperishable grace of his prose.

—Anthony Wolff
Truro, Mass.
June 1973

The Person and the Place

by Susan Flader

Country

We are interested in the convergence of a person and a place—
a person who has come to be regarded as a prophet in the evolution of a new relationship between man and land, and a place little known and undistinguished save as it stimulated in that person and others a heightened sensitivity and deepened respect for the larger community of life. It was a coming together in maturity. Aldo Leopold was well past the midpoint of his life when he came to the sand area of central Wisconsin, already a forester, wildlife manager and conservationist of national repute. And the sand counties were older still, their long history intimately involved with the geologic and human history of the continent. Leopold encountered the sand counties first as a professional land manager, seeking through new tools of public policy and new techniques of resource management to redress the balance of nearly a century of frontier exploitation. His acquisition of a worn out, abandoned sand farm in 1935 initiated a different relationship with the land, at once more personal and more universal. From his own direct participation in the life of the land he came to a deeper appreciation of the ecological, ethical, and esthetic dimensions of the land relationship, and from that experience evolved a sense of place that required a word richer than land. He called it country.

"There is much confusion between land and country," Aldo Leopold once wrote. "Land is the place where corn, gullies, and mortgages grow. Country is the personality of land, the collective harmony of its soil, life, and weather." Geographers referred to the "landscape," but for Leopold the word landscape was too small. Ecologists had a bigger word, "biota," meaning the community of animals and plants integrated with soils and weather in a particular place, and Leopold himself had spoken for a biotic view of land; yet "biota" would not do either, for it was "one of those cold and clammy fictions by which science seeks to separate truth from beauty."

What Leopold was trying to get at was the imponderable essence of certain places, that capacity of certain landscapes to quicken the pulse of the beholder. But was it a quality of the land itself or of the person? Leopold never answered this question directly, but clearly he was dealing with the interaction between a person and a place, and this implies a quality in both. To characterize lands capable of stimulating such a reaction he would use "country," taking the sense of the word as he heard it used by cowmen, naturalists, hunters, "and other artists."

Leopold knew that his taste for country differed markedly from that of most people. As a young forester visiting the Sierra Nevada for the first time and viewing the spectacular rocks and falls of Yosemite National Park he had written home, "I can't say whether it was more pleasure to see Yosemite than pain to see the way most people see it. It's a struggle for me sometimes to play ball with the crowd at all." He appreciated more subtle aspects of the country than most: "The tourists all gape at Yosemite but what none of them see is the fifty miles of foothills on the way in. They are almost a relief after the highly frosted wedding-cake (and the wedding-guests) on the other end. Especially the quail, and the live oaks 'joyously uttering dark green leaves.'"

How to characterize the motive power in country had fascinated Leopold at least since his early years in Arizona and New Mexico. The Southwest was built of hulking mountains and rim-rocked canyons, of gnarled junipers, massive pines and sun-soaked meadows; but even more of continuities with history, of daily encounters with moods and weathers, and of wildlife. Leopold's intuition that these elements were fused in an indivisible whole, that the "dead" earth was actually a living being

9

possessed of soul or consciousness and worthy of respect as such, was affirmed in the early 1920s in the philosophy of a Russian mystic, P.D. Ouspensky, whose *Tertium Organum* had just been published in the United States. Ouspensky provided Leopold with the concept of the "numenon"—the inner meaning or imponderable essence of a thing—as contrasted with the "phenomenon," or outward appearance. But Leopold was no mystic. Uncomfortable with Ouspensky's lifeless abstractions, he needed a physical embodiment of the numenon. For Leopold more often than not it was wildlife which somehow fused the various aspects of land into country.

In the 1920s, in the mountain country, it was deer which to Leopold were the quickening agent:

> To the deer hunter or the outdoorsman, deer are the numenon of the Southwestern mountains. Their presence or absence does not affect the outward appearance of the mountain country, but does mightily affect our reaction toward it. Without deer tracks in the trail and the potential presence of deer at each new dip and bend of the hillside the Southwest would be, to the outdoorsman, an empty shell, a spiritual vacuum.

Two decades later, it was the remembered howl of the wolf "tingling" in his spine that expressed the essence of the place. "Those unable to decipher the hidden meaning know nevertheless that it is there," he wrote, "for it is felt in all wolf country, and distinguishes that country from all other land." Or again, remembering back thirty years to life in Arizona bounded on the far horizon by the pale blue hulk of Escudilla, his lasting impression was not so much of the mountain itself as of its old grizzly. The only place from which you did not see the mountain was on top of it, he recalled. But up there "you could feel it. The reason was the big bear."

The wolf and the grizzly were gone now from the southwestern mountains, "varmints" exterminated by the sons of pioneers to make the ranges safe for cows and deer and men. With their passing something had gone out of the place. Deer abounded, free from fear of wolves, but no longer did they kindle in Leopold that sense of country. Over the years he had come to understand both the destructive potential of too many deer and the function of predators in trimming their prey to the available range. For Leopold the wolf and the grizzly had come to symbolize the integrity of the mountain ecosystem and the continuity of its life processes. Millenia of geologic and evolutionary time had built the mountains and established their living community, continually elaborating and diversifying its food chains, or energy channels. By lopping the large carnivores from the apex of the biotic pyramid, man was making food chains shorter and less complex and thereby disorganizing the system. The howl of the wolf and the incredible tracks of the big bear stimulated a healthy fear—that fear in the individual which is a component of respect for the whole.

Aldo Leopold's deepened appreciation of ecological integrity—his conviction of a relationship between ecological diversity and the stability of the land organism—gave him a new, more objective basis for an ethic grounded in the science of ecology. His biotic view of land led him to the concept of land health. No longer could he dismiss land as simply the place where corn, gullies, and mortgages grow. Land was "a fountain of energy flowing through a circuit of soils, plants, and animals," and health was the normal circulation of energy through the various channels of the system, the capacity of the land organism for internal self-renewal. Overall, land was remarkably resilient, but different lands could stand different degrees of use or abuse by man. Some lands were inherently fragile or poor, less capable of sustaining violent alteration and returning a profit to mechanized man without undergoing a progressive degradation. Hence the need for objective criteria to guide man in his relations with the land. As a start, Leopold asserted that "a thing is right when it tends to preserve the integrity, stability, and beauty of the biotic community. It is wrong when it tends otherwise."

These values—integrity, stability, and to a certain extent beauty—are community values, capable of being generalized to an ethic. They are developed in Leopold's essay, "The Land Ethic," which is the capstone of *A Sand County Almanac*. Although the other essays in the book were written over at least a decade and about experiences during forty years of adult life, Leopold consciously selected and arranged them to promote

Central sand counties area.

perception toward a land ethic. Thus it was that in one of those painful choices sometimes forced upon a writer, he apparently felt compelled to abandon any philosophical discussion of his own subjective concept of "country" in favor of the more objective concept he had developed of "land" and the community values implicit in a land ethic.*

Yet perception is a capacity of the individual, and *Sand County Almanac* is an intensely personal book in which Leopold expresses his own feeling for the motive power in land—his own sense of country. "The experience of country is solitary in proportion to its intensity—gregarious in proportion to superficiality," he had written in an essay on "Country" omitted from *Sand County Almanac.* And again, "In country, as in people, a plain exterior often conceals hidden riches, to perceive which requires much living in and with."

Leopold's country was the sand area of central Wisconsin, the setting of his river bottom farm. Cutover, plowed up, worn out, abandoned, a sandy wasteland baring its history of human suffering and neglect. But despite its conspicuous poverty, or perhaps because of it, one could still flush a partridge or a covey of quail, contemplate at nose-length a tiny Draba, listen for the telltale peent of a dancing woodcock, or chance upon a wahoo flaming rose against a gray October sky. For Leopold it was "lean, poor land, but rich country."

Sand County Backwaters

The sand counties of central Wisconsin are a flat land, and old. They are a legacy of sands slowly settling in the shallow Cambrian sea which covered the interior of the continent half a billion years ago. These sands were compacted, cemented, and capped by limestones and dolomites during subsequent transgressions of the Paleozoic seas, only to be exposed by intervening eons of erosion, then reworked and redeposited by

---

*One of Leopold's unpublished essays on "Country" was later included in *Round River: From the Journals of Aldo Leopold,* brought out by Luna B. Leopold some years after his father's death. The essay was subsequently included with a few others in a new section, "A Taste for Country," sandwiched into an enlarged edition of *Sand County Almanac* published by Oxford Press in 1966 and later issued in paperback by Ballantine Books. All references to *Sand County Almanac* in this essay are to the original version (Oxford Press, 1949).

meltwaters of the great glaciers which receded from the region a scant ten thousand years ago.

There were mountains once, ancient layers of sandstone uplifted, folded and metamorphosed into massive ranges of quartzite more than a billion years ago in the dim reaches of Precambrian time. But these had been worn down to a plain, save for a few isolated nubbins, by the time the Cambrian seas covered the land. The densest, most resistant, and therefore most extensive remnant of those quartzite mountains was the Baraboo syncline, a twenty-five-mile oval at the south end of the present-day sand area; but this too was submerged and buried by the sands and shells of the Paleozoic seas.

Then, three hundred million years ago, the landmass gently warped upward and spilled the last ocean from the state. Through all the intervening years of geologic and biologic evolution, Wisconsin has been part of a stable landmass gradually bequeathing its mantle of soil and rock to other seas. While the Appalachians were uplifted in the East, then the huge Rocky Mountain cordillera and finally the youthful Sierra in the West, Wisconsin eroded seaward. The scale trees, giant ferns, and conifers that evolved and flourished in the late Paleozoic and accumulated in mid-continent basins to form the coal fields of a later day undoubtedly grew in Wisconsin too and helped to hold the soil and retard its seaward wash. Yet the net result of eons was to wear away thousands of feet of sediments overlying the Cambrian sandstone in central Wisconsin and with them all trace of three hundred million years of life. These sediments were carried southward by the ancestral Wisconsin River, which also helped exhume the Baraboo quartzite and then slowly over the eons cut itself a canyon through the rock. Devil's Lake, that canyon is called today.

Then came the Ice Age: A million years which saw four major glacial incursions. We know most about the last episode—the Wisconsin stage—which began seventy thousand years ago and lasted sixty thousand, a series of advances and retreats of a multi-lobed ice sheet. It was the Green Bay lobe of the Cary substage of the Wisconsin glaciation, fed by the snows of Labrador, that moved down out of the northeast a mere fifteen thousand years ago and molded the character of this region. The ice stopped in its advance about a third of the way across the sand

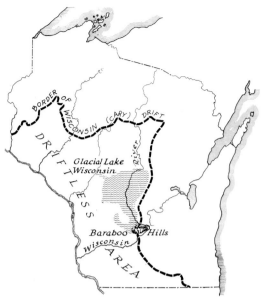

Sand Country landforms.

13

counties, dumping its load of gravel and rock in a north-south heap. The remainder of the area and the entire southwestern portion of Wisconsin has been known for years as the Driftless Area, an island of seemingly unglaciated terrain bounded on all sides by moraines, drumlins, eskers, kames and other evidences of the ice. Although scientists are no longer so sure that the Driftless Area was never covered by ice, the significant point for the sand counties is not the problematical evidence of older drift but the indirect influence of the Cary ice itself on the unglaciated area.

This extra-glacial effect was owing in part to an accident of history and geography in the Baraboo Range, which is now the core of the new Ice Age National Scientific Reserve. The Cary ice, crawling from the east up onto the syncline and slowed perhaps by the steep ascent, was stopped in its advance—probably by the lack of new snow in far-off Labrador—at precisely the point where the ancient Wisconsin River had laboriously cut its channel through the quartzite. Here at Devil's Lake Canyon the glacier dumped its debris.

The saga of the Baraboo Range holds such fascination that it tends to obscure the more prosaic history of the sand county backwaters. When the debris-laden ice dammed up the outlet of the Wisconsin River through the Baraboo quartzite it created

a huge lake, Glacial Lake Wisconsin, over eighteen hundred square miles, covering parts of five counties in central Wisconsin. Glacial meltwaters rushing into this lake from the north and east dropped their gravels near shore and sent their loads of sand and clay in suspension far out across the bed of the lake. Waves pounded away at the outlying islands of quartzite and sandstone, adding still more sands to the lake and leaving isolated buttes, mounds, castellated bluffs, and pinnacles rising from a level marshy plain when the waters receded.

Glacial Lake Wisconsin was not long-lived. The halting of the ice at Devil's Lake was a sign that the climate had already moderated and the ice would soon begin its retreat. Meltwaters that filled the lake soon began draining to the northwest and then later in the old southerly direction. The new Wisconsin River rapidly cut itself a gorge through the weak Cambrian sandstone at the now-heralded Wisconsin Dells and soon found a new course around the east flank of the Baraboo Hills across the flat swampy plain known from the time of the earliest French explorers as The Portage. Here the Wisconsin River on its way to the Mississippi flows within a mile and a half of the Fox River, which drains northeastward to Green Bay and the St. Lawrence. But again, the historical romance of the Fox-Wisconsin portage and the highly touted wonders of the Dells, like the saga of the Baraboo, overshadow the story of the glacial lake bed to the north.

We think of the Ice Age as we think of the ice-covered Arctic today—cold, lifeless, and forbidding. But we forget that we are still living in an ice age, and that virtually all of the species of plants and animals that we know today, including our human predecessors on the North American continent, lived through it. Indeed, historians of climate tell us that the difference in mean annual temperature between periods of glacial advance and glacial decay may have been as little as four or five degrees centigrade; in mid-latitude regions such as Wisconsin, the winters may actually have been milder at the height of the Ice Age than they are now, though the summers were probably somewhat cooler. Radiocarbon-dated remains of charcoal fires and quartzite clovis points, together with plant and animal remains, suggest that early man was in the Driftless Area during the Cary ice, roaming a forest of mixed hardwoods with oak and pine, spruce and fir, and encountering—perhaps hunting—mammoths and mastodons, woodland musk-ox, giant beaver, as well as most of the animals of our own day. Plants, animals, and man moved out rapidly to recolonize lands newly freed of glacial ice and water. There is evidence in fact that the forests grew right up to the edge of the retreating ice and even in the dirt on top of it.

The record of this recolonization and of subsequent environmental changes may be read in the post-glacial peat. Low-lying areas of less porous sands or clay, whether in the lake bed or in the rolling glacial topography to the east, trapped receding meltwaters and subsequently filled with organic matter to become the peat bogs and marshes of the present day. The largest of these is the Great Swamp of Central Wisconsin, lying in the bed of the glacial lake and two-fifths the size of Rhode Island. Other marshes have more romantic names—Roche à Cri, Buena Vista, Pilot Knob, Endeavor, Germania. From fossil pollen grains layered in the peat, scientists have extracted a continuous record of vegetation revealing numerous minor fluctuations. In general, though, the pollen shows a rapid post-glacial decline in spruce and fir and an increase in mixed hardwoods and pine, then in oak and grass indicative of a warmer, drier climate and perhaps also of disturbance by fire. These changes in climate and vegetation were accompanied by changes in animal populations as well. Some of the large mammals like mastodons became extinct in the millenia following the ice, though there is little agreement on the reasons why, but other species such as deer, moose, and elk became more abundant.

What impressed Aldo Leopold most about the record in the peat was not the fluctuations from place to place and time to time but the astonishing stability of the biota—its resilience, its capacity to adjust internally and to persist through millenia as a balanced community, substantially unimpaired despite recurring exigencies. Even on the poor sands of central Wisconsin fertility accumulated faster than it washed away, accompanied, as both cause and effect, by the diversification of flora and fauna.

Central Wisconsin is richly diverse—despite or perhaps because of the poverty of its sands—owing in large part to its position at a boundary between two floristic provinces: the prairies, oak savannahs and southern hardwoods to the south and the pine savannahs, conifer-hardwoods and elements of boreal forest in the north. The preeminent student of the vegetation of Wisconsin, Leopold's friend and colleague, John T. Curtis, described this boundary as a "tension zone"—a band ten to thirty miles wide running diagonally southeast across the state and marking both the northern limit of many southern species and the southern limit of many northern species. Some botanists consider the entire sand area as a widened part of the tension zone, its sands accentuating differences in moisture content and temperature, its low-lying glacial lake beds and river bottoms more prone to frosts, its nutrient-poor acid soils preventing any one species from taking over. The result is an intermingling of species from north and south.

This zone of botanical overlap has shifted over time in response to climatic changes, yet it has persisted throughout the past ten thousand years. It reached the peak of its northward extension, some forty to sixty miles north of its present location, perhaps five thousand years ago, by which time Wisconsin's Old Copper people had hammered complicated implements of native copper not to be rivaled for thousands of years by cultures in Egypt and the Tigris Valley. Thereafter the climate became somewhat cooler and wetter and the tension zone and all its species retreated to approximately their present position. While for particular individuals existence at the limits of their range

entails great risk, for the community as a whole the remarkable diversity of such a zone provides greater resiliency and opportunity for adjustment to change.

This resiliency probably characterized aboriginal human communities in central Wisconsin as well. The woodland peoples who inhabited the area from before the time of Christ until the coming of the French explorers were mostly hunter-gatherers who lived in small nomadic bands and followed the animals from day to day, season to season, century to century. They also fished, made maple sugar, and gathered wild rice; and some of them, especially during periods of more favorable climate, raised corn, beans, and squash in small garden plots along the rivers. But they were not as dependent on agricultural crops as other peoples further to the south. Thus, when highly developed societies of corn farmers at Cahokia (near St. Louis) and elsewhere in the Mississippi heartland collapsed at a time of rapid climatic deterioration around 1200 A.D., the mixed agricultural and hunting cultures of Wisconsin may simply have shifted to a greater reliance on hunting. The deer, elk, and bear which provided much of the meat in their diets were animals especially adapted to the prairie-forest tension zone.

It is possible that the central sand area with its prairie-forest transition belt may have been so rich in animal life and so strategically located that it could not be held as the exclusive terrain of any one group of native people, but rather served as the hunting grounds of several different groups and as a neutral buffer zone between them. Anthropologist Harold Hickerson has described such a buffer region along the tension zone in western Wisconsin and Minnesota during the fur-trade era, separating the Chippewa on the north from Santee Sioux to the south. Both tribes depended for their subsistence on the deer which abounded in the transition belt, and the inability of either tribe to control the area thus prevented overkill not only of deer but of fur-bearing animals as well. Among the tribes who undoubtedly hunted in the central sand region both before and during the fur-trade era are the Menominee, oldest known Indian residents of the state, and the Winnebago, Siouan-speaking peoples who moved into Wisconsin from the middle Mississippi Valley several centuries before white contact and settled in agricultural villages to the east and south of the sand counties.

We know that around 1600 the Winnebago dispersed into small hunting bands and moved westward into southern and central Wisconsin, where they followed the practice of "firing" the forests to produce conditions more favorable for game. But why they left their agricultural villages remains uncertain. Were they displaced by all the dispossessed eastern tribes—Mascouten, Miami and Potawatomi, Kickapoo, Sauk and Fox, Huron and Ottawa—who sought haven in Wisconsin after 1600? And why were those tribes on the move? It is usually assumed that these dislocations were the result of white settlement and the fur trade. But another factor may also have been involved—a rather dramatic deterioration of climate around 1600 similar to that of about 1200, ushering in a period of severe winters and cooler, wetter summers known to European climatologists as "the Little Ice Age." Whatever the complex of causes, central Wisconsin became increasingly important as a hunting area for a large number of tribes. That the Indians managed to sustain not only themselves but the fur trade during more than two centuries of white pressure and cultural dislocation speaks eloquently for the resilience of both the peoples and the lands they hunted.

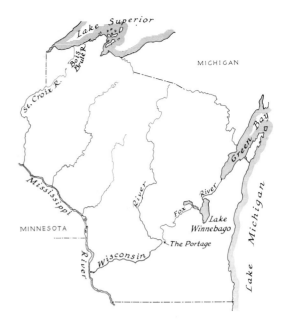

Routes of the explorers.

For all their importance to the Indians, the hunting grounds of central Wisconsin remained unknown to the whites for nearly two centuries after Jean Nicolet greeted the Winnebagos in 1634 on the shores of Green Bay. Louis Jolliet and Father Jacques Marquette made the first officially recorded traverse of Wisconsin via the Fox-Wisconsin waterway in 1673, and thus became the first whites to describe the area. Yet they were only skirting the edges of the sand country.

Within a decade both Robert Cavelier, Sieur de la Salle, and Daniel Greysolon, Sieur du Lhut, had trading parties on the Mississippi and were contending for control of the Fox-Wisconsin route. LaSalle had arrived by way of Chicago and the Illinois river and du Lhut by way of the Brule-St. Croix route from Lake Superior, but the easiest route of all between the Great Lakes and the Mississippi—passable by canoes at high water even without unloading—was the Fox-Wisconsin link forged by the Green Bay lobe of the Cary ice. As the glacier butting against the Baraboo Range had left the sand counties in its backwaters, so also did the Fox-Wisconsin portage route, famed passageway of explorers and fur traders for nearly two centuries.

19

The change came with white settlement. Until 1820 the lands west of Lake Michigan were Indian country. In the 1820s, however, whites pushed into southwestern Wisconsin, lured by rich veins of lead in the Galena dolomite of the driftless hill land. In 1825 the government called Wisconsin Indians to a great intertribal council at Prairie du Chien in order to fix boundaries between the various tribes, as a prelude to negotiating with the tribes piece-meal for cession of their lands. The Winnebago, Chippewa, Ottawa, and Potawatomi ceded lands in the lead region in 1829, and the Black Hawk massacre of 1832 persuaded Indians to turn over the rest of their holdings south and east of the Wisconsin and Fox Rivers. Government surveyors worked the area during 1832-36 and within a decade most of the best lands were taken up by settlers or speculators.

Winnebago, Menominee, and Chippewa Indians meanwhile had retreated to more remote portions of their former territory in central and northern Wisconsin. In 1828, at the request of John Jacob Astor of the American Fur Company, a military post was established near the Indian agency house at The Portage to deal with the recalcitrant Winnebagos. White pine logs, cut on an island some miles upstream by U.S. troops under the command of Lt. Jefferson Davis, were floated down the Wisconsin the following spring to build Fort Winnebago, thus initiating the logging era on the Wisconsin River. In the next decade private entrepreneurs, stimulated by the heavy demand and high price of lumber in the newly opened prairie counties downstream, took up nearly all the available waterpower sites on the central reach of the Wisconsin River for sawmills. The lumber boom was on, and the Indians—and the waning fur trade they supplied—would have to give way to the whites. The Indians were forced to cede their remaining lands in the state in treaties of 1837 and 1848. In the 1850s the Chippewa and Menominee were able to bargain for reservations in small portions of their original homeland. But the Winnebago, rounded up four times by soldiers, kept returning to their sand county hunting grounds.

Pioneer settlers moved into central Wisconsin after the last

Indian cession in 1848, the year Wisconsin achieved statehood. The firstcomers claimed the better soils of the glaciated prairies and oak openings to the east; later arrivals had to make do with the successively sandier, less fertile lands farther west.

Among the earlier arrivals were Daniel Muir and two of his young sons, John and David, who had left Dunbar, Scotland, for the New World in February 1849. Daniel Muir had intended to head for the forests of Upper Canada, John Muir recalled more than half a century later in his *Story of my Boyhood and Youth* (1913), but he was persuaded by other emigrants on the voyage over that the land in the States was as good as in Canada and easier to clear for cultivation. In Buffalo a grain dealer told him that most of the wheat he handled came from Wisconsin, and this information drew Muir to the edge of the settled land in the sand country north of The Portage. Muir selected a quarter section of land—one hundred and sixty acres—four miles from the nearest neighbor and quickly built a shanty of oak logs.

"To this charming hut, in the sunny woods, overlooking a flowery glacier meadow and a lake rimmed with white water-lilies," John Muir reminisced, "we were hauled by an ox-team across trackless carex swamps and low rolling hills sparsely dotted with round-headed oaks." No sooner did they arrive than the boys discovered a blue jay's nest, complete with green eggs

and beautiful birds, and then a bluebird's and a woodpecker's nest, and frogs and snakes and turtles—"Oh, that glorious Wisconsin wilderness!" They marvelled at the newness and freshness of it all, at the "extravagant abounding, quivering, dancing fire" of millions of lightning-bugs on a sultry evening, the *boomp, boomp, boomp* of partridge drumming, the mysterious winnowing of jacksnipe spiraling high overhead and plummeting earthward, the great long-legged sandhill cranes on the meadow.

But there was work to be done, the hard work of making a farm, and Daniel Muir was a severe taskmaster. There were trees to chop and brush to cut down and burn, tough prairie sod to turn with the plow, taking care to dodge all the stumps which later would have to be dug and chopped out to make way for the McCormick reaper. There were wheat, corn, and potatoes to plant and then to hoe, stovewood to chop, fence rails to split, and a new frame house to finish before the rest of the family arrived from Scotland in the fall. Then the harvest: cutting, shocking and husking the Indian corn, cradling, raking and binding the wheat, stacking, threshing. "It often seemed to me," wrote John Muir, "that our fierce, over-industrious way of getting the grain from the ground was too closely connected with grave-digging....Men and boys, and in those days even women and girls, were cut down while cutting the wheat." He was convinced

that all the plowing, chopping, splitting, grubbing, hoeing and threshing of his childhood stunted his growth.

To get cash for wheat—fifty cents a bushel—it had to be hauled by wagon to Milwaukee, a hundred miles away. In the first years they got up to twenty-five bushels an acre, but within five years the soil was so exhausted that they got only five or six bushels even in the better fields. Yet Daniel Muir doggedly cleared more fields, planted them to wheat and then to corn, built more fences and outbuildings for cattle and pigs and horses. And then, after eight years of effort, "after all this had been victoriously accomplished, and we had made out to escape with life," John Muir recalled, he bought a half-section of wild land five miles away and started all over again. To what end?

Muir recalled a discussion his father had once had with a neighbor who was concerned about the Indians having been robbed of their lands and their means of livelihood. "Father replied that surely it could never have been the intention of God to allow Indians to rove and hunt over so fertile a country and hold it forever in unproductive wildness, while Scotch and Irish and English farmers could put it to so much better use." But the neighbor countered that the farming practices of the immigrants, many of whom had been mechanics, merchants, or servants in the old country, were themselves rude, unprofitable, and devastating to the land; how should they now like to be dispossessed by trained and talented farmers using the same argument, that God could never have intended inexperienced immigrants to occupy lands on which scientific farmers could raise five or ten times as much? In Muir's view the neighbor had the better part of the argument.

More to the point: Why toil and sweat and grub oneself into an early grave on a quarter section of land, trying in vain to get rich, when a comfortable enough living could be won on a fourth as much land, and time gained to "get better acquainted with God" and maybe even enjoy life? "No other wild country I have ever known extended a kinder welcome to poor immigrants," Muir remarked. There were bur oaks to build a log house; rich prairie soils which gave exhuberant yields of corn, potatoes, garden vegetables, and melons, at least in the first years; and wild hay for cows and oxen growing in meadow and marsh. Prairie chickens and bobwhite quail and geese frequented the wheat and corn fields and became more abundant as the fields increased. Along the Fox River not far away were wild-rice marshes which harbored "millions" of ducks. Indians came to harvest the rice and ducks in the fall, and the Yankees also feasted royally on fowl; though industrious Scotch immigrants like the Muirs, to John's dismay, seldom found time to hunt. There were deer too, attracted to the farm fields along the prairie-forest border, but again it was the Indians and the Yankees who hunted. In early spring the country offered pasque-flowers, pushing into purple bloom on fire-charred windswept hills, then the wondrous "lady's-slippers" or "Indian moccasins," the lilies, butterfly weed, asters, and "other fine plant people." The sunny woods and meadows yielded strawberries, the bogs and marshes cranberries and dewberries and huckleberries. Hickory trees gave both syrup and nuts, if one were willing to compete with sapsuckers and squirrels and, on certain memorable occasions, with incredible storms of passenger pigeons.

It was a poor land for making money, as John Muir remembered it, but rich country for living.

About the time John Muir left the sand country to exhibit his hand-carved hickory clocks at the state agricultural fair in Madison and make his own way in the world, the most noted historian of the pioneer experience was born in the bustling river town of Portage. Son of a newspaper editor and local Republican wheelhorse who had drifted west to Portage from upstate New York, and of a pioneer schoolmarm from the tiny village of Friendship in the heart of the sand country, Frederick Jackson Turner grew up in a fluid frontier society.

Portage was the hub of transportation arteries that penetrated the sand counties toward frontiers farther to the north and west. Past the Turner home ran the "Old Pinery Road" to the upper Wisconsin, supply line for the logging camps in the days before the railroads. Through the streets of Portage rumbled the covered wagons of the emigrant trains, heading west from the worn out wheatlands of southern Wisconsin to the virgin prairies of Minnesota and the Dakotas. As the emigrants left town they traveled some miles along the river dotted with rafts of lumber bound for Mississippi River railheads and prairie markets beyond. The rafts were white pine cut from the sandy streambanks of central and northern Wisconsin and piloted over a succession of dangerous rapids, bars, and falls on the wild Wisconsin, longest and most perilous of the pinery streams. Wisconsin by the 1870s had lost its supremacy in wheat, and pine was now king. Of an estimated one hundred and thirty billion board feet of white pine on Wisconsin's twenty million acres of conifer-hardwood forest when Turner was a boy, less than one percent would still be standing when Aldo Leopold arrived in the state half a century later.

On the rail line from Chicago and Milwaukee, Portage won out as a terminus of the Wisconsin Central Railroad, heading north through the pineries to Lake Superior. Turner traveled the line with his father in 1877, the year it was completed. His father was part railroad promoter and land speculator, like many frontier boosters of the time, and he used the pages of his newspaper to dispel the image of central and northern Wisconsin as a swampy, sandy, sterile wasteland. What impressed the Turners most as they traveled north was not the unbroken forest or even the logging camps and thriving sawmills at intervals along the tracks, but rather the innumerable "choppings" where pioneer homesteaders and others who had bought lands from the railroad company were starting to open up farms and make homes. The greatest wealth of this part of the state, Turner's father maintained, was not in the pines but in the agricultural lands which would succeed them, lands which would undoubtedly become the finest wheat growing portion of the state.

The Wisconsin of Frederick Jackson Turner's boyhood was a rapidly evolving social order. Old Fort Winnebago still stood, a reminder of the dying days of the fur trade. As Turner roamed the streams and lakes of the sand country in quest of trout or pickerel or bass, he occasionally chanced upon Indians who had escaped their seemingly inevitable fate of removal to reservations. He also observed later stages of succession as the earliest white settlers moved on west, nudged along by newer arrivals from Germany, Scandinavia, and Britain, and as wheat farming gave way to dairying. In town the changes were even more dramatic—the coming of the railroads, the erection of new commercial establishments and public buildings, the rapid population turnover and the medley of ethnic groups that made local politics ever more complex and fascinating. Everywhere was expansion.

"I am placed in a *new* society which is just beginning to realize that it has made a place for itself by mastering the wilderness and peopling the prairie, and is now ready to take its great course in universal history," Turner wrote to his fiancee in 1887 while a student at the University of Wisconsin. "It is something of a compensation to be among the advance guard of new social ideas and among a people whose destiny is all unknown. The west looks to the future, the east to the past."

From this sense of being part of a society oriented to the future Frederick Jackson Turner was to forge a stunning explanation of the American past. The Turner frontier thesis, as it is called—after Turner's most important statement of the theme in an 1893 address, "The Significance of the Frontier in American History"—dominated American historical thought for the first quarter of the twentieth century, spawning a "frontier school" of scholarship. Since then the thesis has been subjected to repeated criticism and revision, but the quantity and intensity of the discussion is in itself tribute to the resonant chord Turner struck in the American mind.

"The peculiarity of American institutions," Turner pointed out, "is the fact that they have been compelled to adapt themselves to the changes of an expanding people—to the changes involved in crossing a continent, in winning a wilderness, and in

developing at each area of this progress out of the primitive economic and political conditions of the frontier into the complexity of city life." The driving force of American development was the existence of an area of free land, and the existence of free land exerted a transforming influence not only on the frontier but on the entire nation and even on the Old World.

Turner was telling Americans what they already intuitively knew about themselves. Thomas Jefferson had stated the belief of an earlier generation that a nation of independent farmers was the greatest assurance of democracy and that a happy republic, free from the social strife of Europe, would endure so long as there was the possibility of expanding to new lands. At the same time he realized that the very existence of free lands, especially in view of the scarcity of capital and labor, made destructive exploitation of the land almost inevitable. There was a paradox here; but Americans, if they thought about it at all, were characteristically willing to charge off the costs of exploitation against the benefits of individualism and democracy and and national pride.

But now the frontier was drawing to a close. According to a report of the U.S. census of 1890, it was no longer possible to draw a line of frontier settlement on the map. Whether one affirmed the pioneer values, as Turner did, or questioned them, perhaps in the manner of John Muir, there was still the nagging problem: What happens to America when there is no more free land?

Turner called it the problem of the West: "A people composed of heterogenous materials, with diverse and conflicting ideals and social interests, having passed from the task of filling up the vacant spaces of the continent, is now thrown back upon itself, and is seeking an equilibrium....The forces of reorganization are turbulent and the nation seems like a witches' kettle." What was the nature of the equilibrium? The farthest he would venture, in a rather remarkable bit of provincialism, was to suggest that the Old Northwest—Turner's Wisconsin and neighboring states—held the balance of power and was the battlefield on which the issues of American development would be settled. This gave him cause for hope, for he had confidence that this "Center of the Republic," with its commitment to what was original and good in its western experience and its openmindedness to change, could be trusted to strike a wise balance between contending ideals. But the problem of the West was not easy of solution—it meant "nothing less than the problem of working out original social ideals and social adjustments for the American nation."

Thus, ironically, through Turner's frontier thesis, the sand country of his boyhood—backwater of continental glaciation and exploration, zone of contention in the age-long battle between prairie and forest, buffer between tribe and tribe—entered the center stage of the nation's history.

After his rise to fame, Frederick Jackson Turner spent part of his career as a professor of history at Harvard. But in June 1924, when he retired from teaching, he returned to the University of Wisconsin to continue his research and writing. Also moving to Madison that summer of 1924, settling by chance in the gray stucco house just two doors west of Turner's Cape Cod bungalow, was another interpreter of the American past with a concern for the shape of its future. Aldo Leopold would experience the sand country at the end of his life, as Turner and Muir did at the beginning of theirs, and draw from it values for a new generation.

Aldo Leopold, Pioneer in Conservation

About the time that Frederick Jackson Turner first realized he was part of a *new* society which had passed from its task of mastering the wilderness and peopling the prairie and was now ready to play its role in world history, Aldo Leopold was born into another segment of that new society in another midwestern river town. Burlington, Iowa, in 1887 was a thriving commercial center of about twenty thousand on the Chicago, Burlington and Quincy Railroad. Here lumber rafted from the Wisconsin pineries was transferred to railroad cars and transformed into houses and barns on the treeless plains. Aldo Leopold's father, son of a German aristocrat who came adventuring to the New World in the 1830s, started work out on the plains, selling barbed wire and roller skates to farmers in Kansas and Nebraska. But when he married the daughter of Charles Starker, a prominent German-educated architect, merchant, banker, and civic leader of Burlington, his father-in-law helped him found a furniture company for the manufacture of fine-quality walnut desks.

Growing up in the big mansion atop Prospect Hill with the Mississippi River flowing from horizon to horizon down below the bluffs, and overhead the wingbeats of millions of migratory waterfowl following the great continental flyway spring and fall, Leopold early acquired his father's and grandfather's contagion for things wild and free. Grandfather Starker was a fine naturalist, and Leopold's father was a sportsman imbued with ethical restraint, who voluntarily stopped shooting waterfowl in the spring, years before it became illegal. With his father, his brothers, or alone, Leopold often walked the railroad tracks downstream until the bluffs opened out into bottomlands teeming with wildlife, or rode the CB&Q across the Mississippi to the duck marshes on the Illinois side, or headed west by train to upland woods and fields for quail and partridge. He wished he had been Daniel Boone, his younger brother recalled. But much as he loved to shoot, he could also take time to observe, and during his years at Lawrenceville Academy in New Jersey and in Sheffield Scientific School at Yale he followed his bent toward field ornithology and natural history.

Though his parents undoubtedly hoped he would return to Burlington to help manage the Leopold Desk Company, Leopold's love of the outdoors drew him instead to an exciting new profession just then sinking its academic roots at Yale and bearing practical fruit in the wilderness West. The art and science of forestry, as developed by the first chief of the U.S. Forest Service, Gifford Pinchot, and a cadre educated principally at the Yale Forest School in the first decade of the 20th century, can be viewed as one of the "original social adjustments" called for by Frederick Jackson Turner in response to the problem of the West. "When the pioneer hewed a path for progress through the American wilderness," Leopold once wrote, "there was bred into the American people the idea that civilization and forests were two mutually exclusive propositions. Development and forest destruction went hand in hand; we therefore adopted the fallacy that they were synonymous. A stump was our symbol of progress." One thinks of Turner and his father riding the Wisconsin Central through the pineries, exalting at the homesteaders' "choppings" and envisioning waving fields of wheat. Pinchot's forestry began with the premise that trees, like wheat, were a crop: it was neither inevitable nor desirable that the nation's forests should disappear, that the plow should everywhere follow the axe. But one did not preserve forests simply by banning the axe. That trees required decades or centuries rather than months to mature was cause not for despair but for farsighted planning and scientific management, to assure that there would be continuous new growth equal to the annual harvest.

Prodded by the threat of timber famine as lumber barons laid waste the Lake States pineries, Congress as early as 1891 gave the President authority to set aside national forest reserves in the western mountains. Although scientific forestry as such was not yet contemplated, the mere establishment of publicly owned reserves marked a sharp break with the century-old policy of deeding all public lands to private interests for settlement and exploitation, and the innovation was met with mounting opposition. It remained for Gifford Pinchot and a small group of federal officials, heartily backed by President Theodore Roosevelt, to sell the American people on the idea of retaining the forests in public ownership "for the permanent good of the whole people," and to demonstrate that the new Forest Service, organized in 1905, was capable of providing efficient, long-term, sustained-yield management. This they accomplished under the banner of "Conservation," a term they appropriated in 1907 to launch a national moral crusade. The new forestry profession was made-to-order for a man like Leopold, who combined a pioneer spirit with social consciousness and a love of nature with managerial acumen.

When he graduated from Yale with a master of forestry degree in June 1909, Leopold already had his orders to report to Albuquerque, headquarters of the new Southwestern District of the Forest Service, embracing the territories of New Mexico and Arizona. At his first assignment, the remote cowtown of Springerville in east central Arizona on the edge of the Apache National Forest, he lost little time in outfitting himself with a horse, saddle, boots, spurs, chaps, ten-gallon hat and all the other accoutrements of the local cow-culture. This was the frontier he had missed in Burlington by more than a generation. The domain of hostile Apaches until the capture of Geronimo in

1886, the mesa and canyon country of the southwestern mountains was one of the last parts of the nation to be settled. Wild Texas longhorns roamed the open ranges, wildlife was as abundant as anywhere in the West though rapidly diminishing, and there were scarcely any roads or other conveniences of civilization.

Leopold thought long and hard about the pioneer experience during his years in the Southwest. He was enamored of the whole thing, attracted to the country, the people, the rough-and-tumble of the times. Yet his training as a forester and his commitment to the conservation idea made him acutely conscious of the enormous costs to the community involved in unrestricted private exploitation of resources. The Forest Service was prepared to deal rationally with the timber resource, but what of the overgrazed watersheds scoured by erosion; of wildlife threatened with extinction by unrestricted hunting and wholesale destruction of habitat; of the wilderness itself, fated to disappear everywhere under the onslaught of mechanized man? Leopold could not confine his concern to the trees, nor did he believe the Forest Service should be so constrained.

Pioneering—the process of so modifying the virgin earth as to render it suitable for building homes and supporting families —he acknowledged as "one of the most meritorious of all human occupations." Reducing the wilderness to possession entailed an incalculable investment of labor, hardship, and sometimes even bloodshed. Hence the community ought to consider whether its methods of conquering the wilderness were efficient methods—whether they produced "a maximum of habitable land for a minimum of effort and suffering." Years of nosing his horse into one washed-out valley after another in the national forests of the Southwest led him to question whether current practices yielded a net gain—whether more land was not lost to erosion than was gained by clearing, fencing, ground-breaking, and irrigating. While one individual was putting a new field under irrigation, another was losing an older field from floods, and a third was causing the floods through misuse of his range. "This scattering of cause and effect and of loss and gain among different owners or industries may give the individual his alibi," Leopold observed, "but it changes not one whit the inefficiency of our joint enterprise in 'developing' the country. We, the com-

munity, are saving at the spigot and wasting at the bunghole, and it is time we realized it."

In a series of speeches and articles, among them one fittingly titled "Pioneers and Gullies," Leopold tallied erosion losses in mountain valleys and compared the economic and social costs with the vaunted "gains" from new federal roads, dams, and reclamation works. To him the conclusion was inescapable that the losses had to be *prevented* rather than merely replaced, and this called for a combination of private obligation and public policy. "The day will come," he predicted, "when the ownership of land will carry with it the obligation to so use and protect it with respect to erosion that it is not a menace to other landowners and the public."

Such an obligation would ultimately have to be enforced, and the costs equitably assessed. But even short of such a massive adjustment in social ideals and public policy, there were basic techniques of erosion control and simple land use policy adjustments that could be inaugurated almost immediately and inexpensively. Leopold devoted a good deal of effort during his years in the Southwest to perfecting and promoting these interim measures. Still, there was the nagging question in his mind whether white Americans, with their engines of violence and their competitive economic system, could maintain a permanent functional civilization in balance with the fragile equilibrium of the arid Southwest.

One small test of man's ability to live in harmony with the southwestern environment, it seemed to Leopold, might be his capacity to maintain viable populations of wildlife. Wildlife was his hobby years before it became his profession, and from his perspective as a forester it seemed to him that civilization need not spell the doom of wildlife anymore than of forests. The conservation idea, the idea of encouraging production by essentially natural means and harvesting on a sustained-yield basis, ought to be applicable to wild game as well as to forests. Leopold's accomplishments in devising and promoting game management techniques and policies not only gave him a national reputation, but also made New Mexico a leader among the states in wildlife conservation.

Just as the pioneer process need not involve wholesale destruction of forests, watersheds, and wildlife, neither ought it eliminate wilderness. In answer to critics who opposed the creation of national forests for fear the timber resource would remain locked up as wilderness, Gifford Pinchot had promulgated the doctrine of "highest use" by which he intended that the forest preserves would be opened up and developed as producing lands. Before long, though, that promise of development had been more than met; so much so that there were few remaining examples of the wilderness which had once engulfed the American continent. The principal of "highest use" now demanded that representative portions of some forests be retained in their wild, roadless condition, Leopold argued, in order to preserve samples of the various natural environments which had shaped the American character as a resource for future generations. Through his efforts, a large portion of the Gila National Forest in southwestern New Mexico was designated as wilderness in 1924, providing an example for the establishment of a nationwide system of wilderness areas.

In his activist concern for watersheds, wildlife, and wilderness, Leopold was probably pushing the Forest Service faster and farther than it was prepared to go. By 1919 he had risen to chief of operations in the Southwestern District, with responsibility for business organization, personnel, finance, roads and trails, and fire control on twenty million acres of national forests. It was the second highest position in the district and Leopold was under considerable pressure to attend to the Service's more utilitarian concerns. He would undoubtedly have preferred greater latitude to follow his special interests, but he saw no chance of his being promoted to district forester, and other job offers all entailed his leaving the Southwest. He finally decided in 1924 to accept a transfer to Madison, Wisconsin, as associate director of the U.S. Forest Products Laboratory, the principal research unit of the Forest Service.

The decision to leave the Southwest must have been one of the most difficult of his life. There was no country anywhere that had such a hold on him, and it must have been years before even Wisconsin's sand counties could begin to fill the void. One has only to read "On Top," "Escudilla," "Song of the Gavilan" and the other southwestern essays in *Sand County Almanac* to sense what the southwestern mountain country meant to him.

Aldo Leopold characteristically made the best of whatever

situation he found himself in, and his four years at the Forest Products Laboratory put that trait to the test. Though he had accepted the position of associate director with the understanding that he would become director within a year, the incumbent stayed on, and Leopold once again was saddled with the administrative load without the freedom to chart new directions. And again it was his special interest in wildlife that saw him through.

Southern Wisconsin was not unlike the Iowa of his boyhood. During his first free weekend after settling in Madison, Leopold and his wife, Estella, headed west to the Wisconsin River to locate promising duck grounds and a place to lease for a hunting camp. That fall he hunted the Wisconsin River bottoms almost every weekend, and on weekdays after work tried his luck on partridges, ducks, and jacksnipe in the woods and marshes nearer Madison. It was probably not until the following spring that he first saw the sand country, on a weekend trout fishing trip to White Creek in Adams County with his son, Luna. That fall the sand country drew him back to hunt. Wood and Juneau counties west of the Wisconsin River gave him his first prairie chicken in the bag, lots of partridge, wild cranberries free for the gathering, abandoned farms for campsites, and an irresistible urge to return.

He still had the desire for a hunting camp nearer home. Farmers thought Leopold's idea of a wild rice pond for the ducks "a gold brick," and real estaters sold shore property "by the front inch," so he ended up leasing a place for his boat on Madison's Waubesa Marsh. The "Swan Cr. Gun Club," he called it on the no-trespassing sign. But a year later another man claimed to be the actual owner, and Leopold lost both his lease and his money. When he finally acquired a hunting camp it was not near Madison but on the Current River in the Missouri Ozarks, where he hunted quail for a week each New Year's with his sons, his brothers, and other friends. There were also summertime canoe trips in the Quetico, and two return visits to the Gila Wilderness for deer hunting—the latter with bow and arrow. Someone at the Forest Products Laboratory had given Leopold a length of yew, launching a whole family of champion archers and bowhunters eager to prove their mettle with handcrafted gear.

In his spare time during the Forest Products Laboratory years Leopold wrote numerous articles on forest and wildlife conservation, continued work on a book on southwestern game, and took an active part in statewide efforts to win passage in 1927 of a cluster of progressive measures for reforestation, rural zoning, and conservation administration.

In 1928 he left the Forest Service to pioneer new territory in conservation. With funding from the Sporting Arms and Ammunition Manufacturers Institute he undertook a two year survey of wildlife habitat and game restoration policy in eight states of the north-central region. The game survey took him to his old stamping grounds in Iowa, Illinois, and Missouri, as well as to unfamiliar areas in Ohio, Indiana, Michigan and Minnesota. It also took him over the length and breadth of his new home state, Wisconsin, and sharpened his focus on the sand counties. Leopold's *Report on a Game Survey of the North Central States* (1931), together with a number of wildlife research projects he helped inaugurate at five universities, not only laid the groundwork for game restoration in the region but confirmed his position as one of the most effective advocates of a new approach to wildlife conservation through scientific research and habitat management. Today he is acknowledged by many in the field as the "father" of the profession of wildlife management in America. His *Game Management* (Scribner's, 1933), written as a text for the new field, is still regarded as a

basic statement of the science, art, and profession of wildlife management.

The early 1930s were bleak years of depression in Wisconsin and the nation—hardly an auspicious time to be launching a new profession and a new career. But for Leopold, who had been unemployed for most of two years while he wrote *Game Management,* the depression provided a rationale for the new profession and a new position. In August 1933 he was appointed to a newly created chair of game management at the University of Wisconsin, supported by an unprecedented five-year grant from the Wisconsin Alumni Research Foundation. The chair was lodged in the university's Department of Agricultural Economics in anticipation of Leopold's work on the problems of land utilization on Wisconsin's cutover, tax-reverted, burned out and eroded lands. The sand counties were a case in point.

Settled in the 1850s, '60s, and '70s during the rapid plunder of the central Wisconsin pines, the sand counties did surprisingly well by their inhabitants as long as the lumber camps lasted. The camps provided ready markets for farm produce and winter jobs for the industrious. But the timber boom passed with the pine and the soils would not sustain wheat. On the glaciated sands of the eastern counties farmers shifted increasingly to dairying, at best a marginal operation in competition with more favorable regions of the state; and at worst, where the sand was loose and too many cows overgrazed the scant vegetation, a "blow-out" to both men and land. West of the moraine, blow-outs came even faster and the shifting dunes grew with the years. Large portions of the central Wisconsin cutovers were never plowed at all but devastated by repeated slash fires which killed new seedlings of white and red pine and encouraged the spread of jack pine and scrub oak "barrens."

Out in the marshes, where land could be bought for fifty cents an acre, farmers from the neighboring hills cleared ever more of the tamarack, or let fire do it, and each summer cut and stacked the new lush growth of wild hay. To Leopold looking back, these haymeadow days seemed the Arcadian age for marsh dwellers: "Man and beast, plant and soil lived on and with each other in mutual toleration, to the mutual benefit of all. The marsh might have kept on producing hay and prairie chickens, deer and muskrat, crane-music and cranberries forever." Such had been John Muir's vision too, but the ambitions of industrious pioneers like his father dictated a different future for the haymarshes. In the dry years of the early 1890s farmers anxious to get ahead tried plowing the haylands for crops and were rewarded with the bountiful yields of any virgin soil. When rains returned to thwart their ambitions, the land boomers, loan sharks, and agricultural college experts came forth with a panacea—ditching and draining. Swamp land costing five dollars an acre could be cleared and drained for ten and then ought to be worth twenty-five, said the agricultural bulletin. Hundreds of thousands of acres in central Wisconsin were organized into districts and drained in the early years of the new century, and practically all of the projects failed. The stored fertility of the marshland was quickly exhausted. Rapidly declining crop yields left farmers saddled with debt, while the depressed water table left dry peat to be consumed by virtually inextinguishable fires. Leopold described such a burn: "Sun-energy out of the Pleistocene shrouded the countryside in acrid smoke. No man raised his voice against the waste, only his nose against the smell. After a dry summer not even the winter snows could extinguish the smoldering marsh. Great pockmarks were burned into field and meadow, the scars reaching down to the sands of the old lake, peat-covered these hundred centuries." Fires ran at will over the sand counties during the 1920s, eating the heart out of abandoned lands. The worst fire year of all was 1930, when three hundred thousand acres of peat were consumed.

By 1933, when Leopold began working on land utilization problems with his new colleagues at the university, less than half the land in any of the sand counties was in farms, and of that very little was actively cultivated. The rest was considered wasteland—weeds, brush, runty jack pine, scrub oak, and raw peat sprouting dense thickets of seemingly worthless aspen. Much of the land had reverted to the counties for non-payment of real estate and drainage taxes. There it reposed, for few would think of buying it. Over the region as a whole, outside of a few scattered cities and towns, there were only eight people per square mile, and fewer in many places. On isolated patches of better soils a few families made a reasonable living, and even on the poorer sands and peat some families managed to eke out a

meager subsistence. But these few were locked in rural isolation without even the most basic social services. "When the pioneers originally came to Wisconsin and began the long, arduous task of clearing the land they were willing to undergo the most rigorous and primitive living conditions, hoping that their efforts would eventually reward them with a better life," Leopold's close friend, the noted land economist George Wehrwein, explained. "They looked forward to the day when the land would be broken to the plow, when roads would exist, when schools and churches would be available, and when communities would stand for the gathering together and satisfaction of human wants." Such hopes surrendered to harsh reality: "Unfortunately in many places there was and is no prospect of such community building no matter how hard the individual pioneers work to attain this end."

It required the deepest depression in American history for people finally to confront, even half-blindly, the consequences of mindless expansion and exploitation, and to undertake, however falteringly, that process of social reorganization which Frederick Jackson Turner called for two generations earlier in "The Problem of the West." When Turner suggested that the Old Northwest would be the battlefield on which the problems of American development would be resolved, he could hardly have dreamed that the very part of that region he knew as a boy would become one of the most blighted areas of the nation and an arena for experiment in social and institutional reorganization.

But within little over a year, from late 1933 to 1934, the course of development in the sand counties was dramatically reoriented. The rapid changes were turbulent and to many the area must have seemed like a witch's cauldron boiling with radical doctrines. Stirring the brew were administrators, technicians, and crews from a legion of new alphabetical agencies created by Franklin D. Roosevelt's New Deal—AAA, CCC, CWA, WPA, FERA, FSA, SES—as well as the old Forest Service and Biological Survey, various divisions of the Wisconsin Conservation Department and other state agencies, university departments, the agricultural extension service and county agents, county and town officials, and maybe even a local citizen or two. Overnight, projects were underway on classification and zoning of land; resettlement of families from sub-marginal farms to areas that might support productive agriculture and a self-sustaining community life; plugging of drainage ditches, construction of dikes, and reflooding of marshlands for wildlife, recreation, and cranberry growing; reforestation of sandy uplands; construction of firebreaks, lookout towers, and roads; and even some planting of game food patches and research on grouse. Out of all this came county forests, a state forest, several state and county parks, including one commemorating John Muir, the Necedah National Wildlife Refuge, the Central Wisconsin Conservation Area, numerous public hunting grounds and state wildlife refuges, not to mention private ventures.

In all this ferment it is impossible to trace the precise influence of individuals like Leopold and his colleague Wehrwein, though they were actively involved with most of the agencies, planning and negotiating, advising and criticizing. Their vision of the future of the sand country, including zoning and resettlement, reforestation and reflooding, was reflected in much of the feverish activity on the land. In his 1929 game survey of Wisconsin, Leopold had proposed state acquisition of some of the tax-reverted land in the sand counties for reforestation, reflooding, and management as combined public shooting grounds and public forests. Early in 1933, before the flurry of New Deal programs, he had proposed a Central Wisconsin Foundation to "pioneer beyond the usual and familiar categories of land use." He hoped to find an economic use for the region's tax-reverted and idle lands, a wildlife crop which could coexist with the scattered farms and forest lands without major capital investment. The sand counties were unique in offering a variety of desirable game for every circumstance—wet or dry, forest or prairie, farm or wilderness. Along with the grouse moors of Scotland, which grossed five million dollars annually, they were a conspicuous exception to the general rule that the size and variety of the possible game crop varies directly with the agricultural value of land, and in that fact lay the special economic value of the sand counties as a wildlife area. Without doubt, the subsequent emphasis on the development of wildlife habitat in federal, state, and university projects can be attributed in large part to the far-reaching influence of Aldo Leopold.

Yet Leopold was profoundly dismayed by much of what he saw happening on the ground: clean-up crews taking out all the brush and hollow snags needed for wildlife food and shelter, road crews silting trout streams and gridironing the wilder expanses with unnecessary fire lanes, planting crews setting out jack pines in huge monotypic blocks. Integrated conservation had been accepted in theory ever since the days of Gifford Pinchot and Theodore Roosevelt, but it took the open money bags of 1933, Leopold wryly observed in a talk on "Conservation Economics," to reveal the ecological and esthetic limitations of "scientific technology," especially as practiced by single-track agencies. Neither he nor any of the proponents of integrated conservation had ever before had enough field labor simultaneously at work on different projects to appreciate fully either the pitfalls or the possibilities. "If the *accouchement* of conservation in 1933 bore no other fruits," he concluded, "this sobering experience would alone be worth its pains and cost." But if trained technicians on public lands found it so difficult to integrate the diverse public interests in land use, what of the private landowner?

The wholesale public expenditures of the New Deal indicated to Leopold that government might be persuaded to pay the bill for the ecological debt incurred by private exploitation and abuse of land. But government conservation, no matter how extensive and well administered, could not possibly go far enough. Wouldn't it make more sense to prevent environmental deterioration by encouraging good land use through demonstration, subsidy, and regulation, rather than to "cure" the abuses after the fact? At issue were two conflicting concepts of the desired end. One seemed to regard conservation as "a kind of sacrificial offering, made for us vicariously by bureaus, on lands nobody wants for other purposes, in propitiation for the atrocities which still prevail everywhere else." The other concept—Leopold's—supported the public program, especially in its teaching and demonstration aspects, but regarded government conservation only as an initial impetus, a means to an end. "The real end," he maintained, "is a *universal symbiosis with land,* economic and esthetic, public and private."

It was in this atmosphere, in the first flush of the New Deal, that Aldo Leopold first voiced his concept of a "conservation ethic." Noting the gradual evolution of ethics from individual to social relationships, he called for the extension of ethical criteria to the third element of the human environment, the land and the plants and animals which grow upon it. The idea had evolved during his boyhood on the Mississippi, his years as a forester in the Southwest, and his early contact with the land use problems of central Wisconsin. But his full expression of a land ethic was the product of another order of experience, his own personal interaction with the land at his sand county shack.

The Shack Experience

Writing in later years, Aldo Leopold explained that he had bought himself a sand farm in an attempt to learn what it was about the sand counties that made destitute families unwilling to pull up stakes and resettle elsewhere, even when exhorted by government officials and baited with favorable credit terms. Though he eventually found an answer—and an equal attachment of his own to the sand country—his original acquisition of the shack had not come about in quite that way.

Among the conservation innovations of 1934 was the State of Wisconsin's first bow-and-arrow deer hunting season. Leopold had been arguing for such a season for years, and his party of eight—four Leopolds and four friends—constituted twenty percent of the archers who took advantage of the opportunity that year. They hunted all five days of the season along river bottoms in the southern sand counties, camping out in a tent, and though they failed to get a deer they saw plenty and had a marvelous time. It was enough to rekindle Leopold's old yen for a hunting camp. Ed Ochsner, one of the party, located an abandoned river bottom farm and Leopold visited it with him for the first time on January 12, 1935.

The only building was a dilapidated chicken-house-turned-cowshed with manure knee deep on the floor. The farmhouse on the side of the hill had burned to the ground some years earlier, leaving only a fieldstone foundation. The island opposite the cowshed had been stripped of timber just a year or so before. The marsh across the road had apparently burned around 1930, the year of the great peat fires. But here the fires had not consumed the peat itself, for the river flooded the marsh each spring and the water table was too high. East of the shed was a corned-out field coming up to sand burs and panic grass, while up the hill to the west the sands were bare and blowing. But it would serve adequately for a hunting camp and it could be leased for a song. What's more, Ochsner reported, the former owner would not mind at all if they wanted to do a little work around the yard or even build a house on the old foundation, so long as they didn't make a mess of the place. For Leopold's purposes the cowshed would suffice, but explaining it to his wife was a little delicate. All that manure.

Ten dollars for a lease, a "sort of" contract signed by the owner, and the Leopolds were ready to go to work: Shovelling manure, building a fireplace, repairing the roof, battening the cracks in the walls. The place must have grown on them, for in early May Leopold wrote Ochsner that he had the notion to buy forty acres or so, provided it was obtainable at a proper price. By May 17 he was owner of eighty acres of river bottom land and a cowshed called "the shack." His first recorded act as a landowner was to plant a food patch for wildlife, and his journal entries that summer, scant as they were, did not fail to mention the height of the sorghum.

The shack was a family enterprise to which each member contributed: Cutting and splitting wood, building birdhouses for martins, screech owls, wood ducks, planting prairie grasses and wildflowers, shrubs and trees. From April to October scarcely a day went by that someone did not plant or transplant something—butterfly weed, tamarack, wahoo and oak, june-grass and sideoats, penstemon and puccoon, pipsissewa and pasques. Starker built grape tangles for the birds, and for the family the one essential outbuilding which he dubbed the "Parthenon." Luna designed a new and better fireplace complete with massive sandstone lintel and handhewn cedar log mantel, rubbed to a mellow sheen. Nina and Carl were avid phenologists, observing and recording the annual order of events in nature—the first bloom of the pasques, the arrival of bluebirds, the fall of ripe acorns. In winter they banded resident birds, including 65290, the feisty little chickadee who regularly bloodied his beak in the trap but outlived all his fellows to be immortalized in *Sand County Almanac*. Even Estella, youngest of the family, had her own project, triumphantly constructing bridges to her secret island. Floods could be counted on to wash out her bridges each spring, insuring more days of happy engineering.

42

For Leopold and his family the shack years were an experience in the slow sensitizing of people to land, the evolution of a sense of country. The shack originally acquired as a hunting camp soon became a "weekend refuge from too much modernity," a place to hike and swim and savor the outdoors, to build with their own hands, to split oak and make sourdoughs in the dutch oven at an open fire, to play guitars and sing and talk and laugh together. It was also a place where one could experience a feeling of isolation in nature—especially if one were an insomniac like Leopold, who habitually arrived "too early" in the marsh. And it offered rich country for the growth of perception. The more woodcock nests they discovered, the more trees and shrubs, grasses and flowers they planted, the more chickadees and nuthatches they got to know—in short the more familiar they became with the place—the more they found to anticipate, to ponder, and to marvel at. The journals of their shack visits reveal an almost exponential increase in recorded observations over the years, and *Sand County Almanac* is eloquent testimony to the meaning and value of the experience.

Most important, the shack offered space enough and time to practice the arts of wild husbandry. A sense of husbandry, said Leopold, "is realized only when some art of management is applied to land by some person of perception." Wild husbandry

offered a substitute for what he termed the "split-rail value" of the pioneer tradition, symbolized by Daniel Boone and characterized by free-for-all exploitation of the land. Like the split-rail tradition, it was a reminder of the elemental man-earth relation, but in addition wild husbandry required ethical restraint in the use of tools, and thus had special cultural value for mechanized man.

Nothing better illustrates Leopold's sense of husbandry than his use of shovel and axe in planting and encouraging his pines. Two thousand, three thousand, sometimes five or six thousand pines a year, every year, Leopold and his family planted in an annual week-long ritual, the spring planting trip. They planted them all by hand with shovels so sharp they sang and hummed in their wrists as they sliced the earth. And they planted them with care, in groves, points and stringers, or interspersed with other trees and shrubs.

But not all of the pines thrived. The first year, 1936, ninety-five percent of the Norways and ninety-nine percent of the whites were killed by the drought within three months of planting. The next summer drought losses were heavy again, even among hand-watered seedlings. Leopold's journals contain cryptic hints of his tribulations: "never plant pines near grape or poison ivy" or "you can't put up brush shelters"—which attract rabbits—"and plant white pine at the same time and place." In one winter rabbits trimmed three-quarters of the white pines planted in the woods. Another winter, deer were the culprits, and in the spring, floods drowned out seedlings on lower ground. To compensate, Leopold planted more pines more thickly. He planted pines in grass or beneath nurse trees, in plowed ground or in furrows. He tried spoon-feeding them fertilizer and mulching with marsh hay. He tried weeding by hand, and surrounding each tree with cardboard to kill the grass, and "desodding"—scalping an area of sod around each tree. He became so fond of the desodding technique that the family figured the time it took him to walk home through his pines, scalping all the way, was equal to the square of the distance. But after all this care he could still lose pines to drought or flood or rabbits or deer or rust or weevils, or get bad planting stock from the nursery to begin with, or have birds alight on the candles and break them off, or vandals cut off the leaders out of sheer meanness. Nevertheless, some of the pines managed to survive and within three years Leopold proudly measured them against little Estella—up to her collar or her nose or the top of her head.

Then came the fires. In November 1941 a campfire got away from a trespassing hunter and burned an area of pines near the shack before it was put out by several of the neighbors. The following March a much larger fire of more mysterious origin burned most of the marsh and all but a few of the pine plantings. All that summer the Leopolds watched their pines dying. Many had been killed outright. Others that looked healthy one week were dead the next. An infestation of powder post beetles spread from fire-killed trees to wounded survivors, so they cut and burned all dead and dying trees. Still the toll mounted. Yet fire brought life as well as death. Willows and aspens, wild plum, sumac and hazel resprouted vigorously; dewberry and blackberry, bluestem and lespedeza increased, and so did ragweed and poison ivy. The next summer Leopold was thrilled to find his first natural reproduction—four young jackpines eight inches high growing in a scalp beside a dead white pine, undoubtedly the legacy of cones opened by fire.

So it went, the husbandry of pines—the painstaking care in planting, the anxious days of weeding, watering, watching, the toll of drought, flood, and fire, rabbit and weevil, the pride in measuring the growth of trees that thrived. There was a special dividend from pines which had overcome such adversity. In the snowy stillness of a midwinter evening "when the hush of elemental sadness lies heavy upon every living thing," there were Leopold's pines standing ramrod straight under their burden of snow, and in the dusk beyond he could sense the presence of hundreds more. "At such times," he wrote, "I feel a curious transfusion of courage."

If the shovel symbolized the planting and care of struggling young seedlings, the axe characterized decisions required of the "husbandman" as his vigorous saplings raced skyward. The 1940s were years of the axe as well as the shovel at the Leopold shack, and the axe-in-hand decisions seemed somehow more difficult, perhaps because of their finality. Where a birch was shading a pine, he usually cut the birch. But what of a veteran oak with pines heading toward its out-thrust limbs? Or a cluster of pines planted close in the hope that one would survive—had they all earned the right to compete for greater glory? A wilderness purist might let the trees fight it out among themselves. But the shack was not pure wilderness, nor was Leopold merely a spectator. The land had been heedlessly ravaged by men who regarded it as a commodity to be used and then abandoned. Leopold, by contrast, regarded himself as a participating citizen of the land community, seeking to restore it to ecological integrity, and he would not shirk the ethical decisions this entailed.

Through a lifetime of observation and experience, of perception and husbandry, Aldo Leopold had clarified his understanding of ecological processes and the fundamental values—integrity, stability, and beauty—that he saw as the basis of a land ethic. But ethical values were a guide for individual decisions, not a substitute for them, and Leopold realized this most keenly when he stood with axe in hand. Conservation, he wrote, "is a matter of what a man thinks about while chopping, or while deciding what to chop. A conservationist is one who is humbly aware that with each stroke he is writing his signature on the face of the land." And then an allowance for the subjective hopes, ideals, affections and convictions of the individual: "Signatures of course differ, whether written with axe or pen, and this is as it should be."

Perception honed in the practice of husbandry engendered in Leopold a profound humility in his use of tools. Through his own decisive participation in the land community he became acutely aware of the innumerable, ofttimes inscrutable factors involved in life and death, growth and decay. Not all pines thrived even with the greatest foresight and care, nor did all industrious pioneers turn a profit on their land, nor did all scientific technologies or all alphabetical agencies inevitably yield progress. Though it took some of the certitude out of individual decisions and individual existence, his sense of country gave Leopold a sense of belonging to something greater than himself, a continuity with all life through time. This intellectual humility rooted in a sense of country led Leopold to appreciate "that all history consists of successive excursions from a single starting-point, to which man returns again and again to organize yet another search for a durable scale of values."

For Aldo Leopold the sand country was such a starting point. It was a backwater refuge from the heedless rush of progress, a setting in geological time which he shared with the sandhill cranes, the pines, and the pasques of lineage more ancient than man. At the shack, through his unique capacity for perception and husbandry, he became a participant in the drama of the land's workings, and he transformed the land as it transformed him.

Both the surface and the depths of Leopold's shack experience he expressed in the essays which now comprise *A Sand County Almanac*. At the urging of his closest friends Leopold began as early as 1941 to seek a publisher for his essays in book form. A succession of publishers turned him down over the years. The essays lacked cohesion, they said, or their ecological and philosophical concepts were too difficult for laymen, or the book would not find a market to warrant using scant wartime allotments of paper. Though undoubtedly discouraged, Leopold continued to write essays, and late in 1947 he sent a much expanded and thoroughly restructured version of the manuscript to still other publishers. By this time he was committed to bringing the book out himself if he had to. But on Wednesday, April 14, 1948, Oxford University Press notified him by long-distance telephone that they would be delighted to publish the book.

Leopold left for his annual spring planting trip two days later a happy man. With him were his wife and his daughter, Estella, a senior at the university and the only one of the five children still in Madison. All shack trips were enchanted, but this time everyone was in especially good spirits. Pasques were blooming, tamarack buds bursting, and chickadees were getting paired up, though one banded chick was still without a mate. Ruffed grouse drummed until dark, woodcocks peented at dusk and continued by moonlight, accompanied by goose music on the marsh. On Monday Leopold picked up the pines, only two hundred whites and two hundred reds, fewer than ever before. He was still recuperating from an operation for tic douloureux and was under heavy strain from an overload of students, so he intended to take it easy that year.

That evening, as the geese started to come back from corn, the three Leopolds dressed in khaki brush-colored clothes and walked out to a bench on one of the aspen islands in the marsh to watch them come in. Just as the sun hit the horizon, geese

began arriving in bunches, coasting in low over their heads or "maple leafing" from a great height, tilting first one wing low and then the other to lose altitude. Leopold with his stubby pencil and little black notebook jotted down all the flock counts—5,5,9,2,3,2,8 and so on to a total of 445. He was trying to check the hypothesis that geese flew in family groups. Yet it was not scientific research that drew the Leopolds into the marsh so much as the pure enjoyment of the performance. A basic human quality was the ability to appreciate simple things which could not be eaten or worn or sold, Leopold had told his daughter while they were sweeping the shack floor one morning, and now as they sat on the bench in the marsh and exchanged glances and nudged each other in their enthusiasm over each new flock that came in she knew what he meant. The geese were "a last bit of real wild life in our time, probably the only quantity of game left in these parts," Leopold said with a touch of nostalgia while he entered the day's notes in the journal back at the shack that evening, as his wife knitted and Estella sat on the doorstep playing the guitar and singing softly.

The next morning Leopold was up by 4:30 a.m. as usual, listening for the daybreak songs of the birds and recording the times and light intensities in his notebook while it was still so dark he had to shape the numbers by feel. Later that morning he planted about a hundred pines with Estella, cleared a trail through the prickly ash to the otter pool and cut some sprouts in the birch row. A pileated woodpecker flew past four times. In the afternoon he and his wife went down to inspect Estella's new bridge, then paddled slowly up the slough in the canoe, putting up wood ducks and bluewings. He went straight to bed after writing his journal entry that evening, and Mrs. Leopold confided to Estella her worry about his tiredness.

Wednesday, April 21 dawned clear, calm and cold at the shack. That morning Leopold counted geese heading outward to corn between 5:15 and 5:40 a.m. His total was 871, more geese than he had ever before counted at the shack. "On our farm we measure the amplitude of our spring by two yardsticks: the number of pines planted, and the number of geese that stop," he had written in his essay "The Geese Return," which he had revised for the book just a month earlier. "Our record is 642 geese counted in on 11 April 1946." April 21, 1948, was a new record, though he did not make note of the fact when he transferred his flock counts to the journal that morning.

The three Leopolds were in high spirits as they busied themselves around the shack after breakfast, repairing all the broken tools which Leopold termed "a disgrace to the outfit." Around 10:30 they spotted smoke coming from the east across the marsh on a light breeze. "Someone's burning his hay meadow," Leopold commented as he continued with his tools. Then suddenly he became very concerned and excited, sent Estella after the Indian fire pump in the shack, tossed buckets and a sprinkling can, coats, gloves and brooms in the car. The three drove east along the birch row a half mile to his new neighbor's farm, where they found a large area already burned and flames in places leaping five to eight feet high. About ten neighbors were there already fighting the blaze with pumps and buckets but it was out of control, moving rapidly toward the goose marsh and the pines beyond. Leopold told Estella to drive to the nearest phone and call the fire department, stationed his wife at the road with a broom to keep the fire from crossing, grabbed the sprinkling can and headed toward the flames.

"Professor Aldo Leopold, Burned Fighting Grass Blaze, Dies" said the headline in the Madison paper that evening. But Aldo Leopold had fought too many fires in his life to be downed by flames. It was a coronary attack, the doctors decided when they heard the circumstances. He had fallen on unburned grass, probably not long after he left his wife and daughter, and the fire had swept lightly over him sometime later.

Aldo Leopold's passing left a void in his family, among his friends, and in the world of conservation thought. But it was a void ultimately filled by the imperishable force of his spirit and by the little book which embodied it. The book contains no panaceas, no blueprints for mass action. It is simply one man's expression of his experience with the land, his sense of country, offered to others who would search in their own way, in their own time and place, for the larger meaning and purpose in life. *Sand County Almanac* was published in 1949 with a new foreword Leopold had written just the month before his death. "There are some who can live without wild things," he had begun, "and some who cannot. These essays are the delights and dilemmas of one who cannot."

Sand
Country

Selections from the writings of Aldo Leopold

Each year, after the midwinter blizzards, there comes a night
of thaw when the tinkle of dripping water is heard in the land.
It brings strange stirrings, not only to creatures abed for
the night, but to some who have been asleep for the winter.
The hibernating skunk, curled up in his deep den, uncurls
himself and ventures forth to prowl the wet world, dragging
his belly in the snow. His track marks one of the earliest datable
events in that cycle of beginnings and ceasings which we call
a year.

Like winds and sunsets, wild things were taken for granted until progress began to do away with them. Now we face the question whether a still higher 'standard of living' is worth its cost in things natural, wild, and free. For us of the minority, the opportunity to see geese is more important than television, and the chance to find a pasque-flower is a right as inalienable as free speech.

These wild things, I admit, had little human value until mechanization assured us of a good breakfast, and until science disclosed the drama of where they come from and how they live. The whole conflict thus boils down to a question of degree. We of the minority see a law of diminishing returns in progress; our opponents do not.

Conservation is getting nowhere because it is incompatible with our Abrahamic concept of land. We abuse land because we regard it as a commodity belonging to us. When we see land as a community to which we belong, we may begin to use it with love and respect. There is no other way for land to survive the impact of mechanized man, nor for us to reap from it the esthetic harvest it is capable, under science, of contributing to culture.

That land is a community is the basic concept of ecology, but that land is to be loved and respected is an extension of ethics. That land yields a cultural harvest is a fact long known, but latterly often forgotten.

All ethics so far evolved rest upon a single premise: that the individual is a member of a community of interdependent parts. His instincts prompt him to compete for his place in that community, but his ethics prompt him also to co-operate (perhaps in order that there may be a place to compete for).

The land ethic simply enlarges the boundaries of the community to include soils, waters, plants, and animals, or collectively: the land....

In short, a land ethic changes the role of *Homo sapiens* from conqueror of the land-community to plain member and citizen of it. It implies respect for his fellow-members, and also respect for the community as such.

We let the dead veteran season for a year in the sun it could no longer use, and then on a crisp winter's day we laid a newly filed saw to its bastioned base. Fragrant little chips of history spewed from the saw cut, and accumulated on the snow before each kneeling sawyer. We sensed that these two piles of sawdust were something more than wood: that they were the integrated transect of a century; that our saw was biting its way, stroke by stroke, decade by decade, into the chronology of a lifetime, written in concentric annual rings of good oak.

It took only a dozen pulls of the saw to transect the few years of our ownership, during which we had learned to love and cherish this farm. Abruptly we began to cut the years of our predecessor the bootlegger, who hated this farm, skinned it of residual fertility, burned its farmhouse, threw it back into the lap of the County (with delinquent taxes to boot), and then disappeared among the landless anonymities of the Great Depression. Yet the oak had laid down good wood for him; his sawdust was as fragrant, as sound, and as pink as our own. An oak is no respecter of persons.

We have cut the core. Our saw now reverses its orientation in history; we cut backward across the years, and outward toward the far side of the stump. At last there is a tremor in the great trunk; the saw-kerf suddenly widens; the saw is quickly pulled as the sawyers spring backward to safety; all hands cry 'Timber!'; my oak leans, groans, and crashes with earth-shaking thunder, to lie prostrate across the emigrant road that gave it birth.

Now comes the job of making wood.

The same logic that causes big rivers always to flow past big cities causes cheap farms sometimes to be marooned by spring floods. Ours is a cheap farm, and sometimes when we visit it in April we get marooned.

Not intentionally, of course, but one can, to a degree, guess from weather reports when the snows up north will melt, and one can estimate how many days it takes for the flood to run the gauntlet of upriver cities. Thus, come Sunday evening, one must go back to town and work, but one can't. How sweetly the spreading waters murmur condolence for the wreckage they have inflicted on Monday morning dates!

There are degrees and kinds of solitude. An island in a lake has one kind; but lakes have boats, and there is always the chance that one might land to pay you a visit. A peak in the clouds has another kind; but most peaks have trails, and trails have tourists. I know of no solitude so secure as one guarded by a spring flood; nor do the geese, who have seen more kinds and degrees of aloneness than I have.

One hundred and twenty acres, according to the County Clerk, is the extent of my worldly domain. But the County Clerk is a sleepy fellow, who never looks at his record books before nine o'clock. What they would show at daybreak is the question here at issue.

Books or no books, it is a fact, patent both to my dog and myself, that at daybreak I am the sole owner of all the acres I can walk over. It is not only boundaries that disappear, but also the thought of being bounded. Expanses unknown to deed or map are known to every dawn, and solitude, supposed no longer to exist in my county, extends on every hand as far as the dew can reach.

During every week from April to September there are, on the average, ten wild plants coming into first bloom. In June as many as a dozen species may burst their buds on a single day. No man can heed all of these anniversaries; no man can ignore all of them. He who steps unseeing on May dandelions may be hauled up short by August ragweed pollen; he who ignores the ruddy haze of April elms may skid his car on the fallen corollas of June catalpas. Tell me of what plant-birthday a man takes notice, and I shall tell you a good deal about his vocation, his hobbies, his hay fever, and the general level of his ecological education.

...farm neighborhoods are good in proportion to the poverty of their floras. My own farm was selected for its lack of goodness and its lack of highway; indeed my whole neighborhood lies in a backwash of the River Progress.

My road is the original wagon track of the pioneers, innocent of grades or gravel, brushings or bulldozers. My neighbors bring a sigh to the County Agent. Their fencerows go unshaven for years on end. Their marshes are neither dyked nor drained. As between going fishing and going forward, they are prone to prefer fishing. Thus on week ends my floristic standard of living is that of the backwoods, while on week days I subsist as best I can on the flora of the university farms, the university campus, and the adjoining suburbs.

The wind that makes music in November corn is in a hurry.
The stalks hum, the loose husks whisk skyward in half-playful
swirls, and the wind hurries on.

   In the marsh, long windy waves surge across the grassy
sloughs, beat against the far willows. A tree tries to argue,
bare limbs waving, but there is no detaining the wind.

   On the sandbar there is only wind, and the river sliding
seaward. Every wisp of grass is drawing circles on the sand.
I wander over the bar to a driftwood log, where I sit and listen
to the universal roar, and to the tinkle of wavelets on the shore.
The river is lifeless: not a duck, heron, marshhawk, or gull
but has sought refuge from wind.

Out of the clouds I hear a faint bark, as of a far-away dog.
It is strange how the world cocks its ears at that sound,
wondering. Soon it is louder: the honk of geese, invisible, but
coming on.

The flock emerges from the low clouds, a tattered banner
of birds, dipping and rising, blown up and blown down, blown
together and blown apart, but advancing, the wind wrestling
lovingly with each winnowing wing. When the flock is a blur
in the far sky I hear the last honk, sounding taps for summer.

It is warm behind the driftwood now, for the wind has gone
with the geese. So would I—if I were the wind.

As in fall, our spring geese make daily trips to corn, but these are no surreptitious sneakings-out by night; the flocks move noisily to and from corn stubbles through the day. Each departure is preceded by loud gustatory debate, and each return by an even louder one. The returning flocks, once thoroughly at home, omit their *pro-forma* circlings of the marsh. They tumble out of the sky like maple leaves, side-slipping right and left to lose altitude, feet spraddled toward the shouts of welcome below. I suppose the ensuing gabble deals with the merits of the day's dinner.

I find it disconcerting to analyze, *ex post facto,* the reasons behind my own axe-in-hand decisions. I find, first of all, that not all trees are created free and equal. Where a white pine and a red birch are crowding each other, I have an *a priori* bias; I always cut the birch to favor the pine. Why?

Well, first of all, I planted the pine with my shovel, whereas the birch crawled in under the fence and planted itself. My bias is thus to some extent paternal, but this cannot be the whole story, for if the pine were a natural seedling like the birch, I would value it even more. So I must dig deeper for the logic, if any, behind my bias.

The birch is an abundant tree in my township and becoming more so, whereas pine is scarce and becoming scarcer; perhaps my bias is for the underdog. But what would I do if my farm were further north, where pine is abundant and red birch is scarce? I confess I don't know. My farm is here.

The pine will live for a century, the birch for half that; do I fear that my signature will fade? My neighbors have planted no pines but all have many birches; am I snobbish about having a woodlot of distinction? The pine stays green all winter, the birch punches the clock in October; do I favor the tree that, like myself, braves the winter wind? The pine will shelter a grouse but the birch will feed him; do I consider bed more important than board? The pine will ultimately bring ten dollars a thousand, the birch two dollars; have I an eye on the bank? All of these possible reasons for my bias seem to carry some weight, but none of them carries very much.

So I try again, and here perhaps is something; under this pine will ultimately grow a trailing arbutus, an Indian pipe, a pyrola, or a twin flower, whereas under the birch a bottle gentian is about the best to be hoped for. In this pine a pileated woodpecker will ultimately chisel out a nest; in the birch a hairy will have to suffice. In this pine the wind will sing for me in April, at which time the birch is only rattling naked twigs. These possible reasons for my bias carry weight, but why? Does the pine stimulate my imagination and my hopes more deeply than the birch does? If so, is the difference in the trees, or in me?

The only conclusion I have ever reached is that I love all trees, but I am in love with pines.

There is much small-talk and neighborhood gossip among pines. By paying heed to this chatter, I learn what has transpired during the week when I am absent in town. Thus in March, when the deer frequently browse white pines, the height of the browsings tells me how hungry they are. A deer full of corn is too lazy to nip branches more than four feet above the ground; a really hungry deer rises on his hind legs and nips as high as eight feet. Thus I learn the gastronomic status of the deer without seeing them, and I learn, without visiting his field, whether my neighbor has hauled in his cornshocks.

It is fortunate, perhaps, that no matter how intently one studies the hundred little dramas of the woods and meadows, one can never learn all of the salient facts about any one of them.

Every profession keeps a small herd of epithets, and needs a pasture where they may run at large. Thus economists must find free range somewhere for their pet aspersions, such as submarginality, regression, and institutional rigidity. Within the ample reaches of the Sand Counties these economic terms of reproach find beneficial exercise, free pasturage, and immunity from the gadflies of critical rebuttal.

Soil experts, likewise, would have a hard life without the Sand Counties. Where else would their podzols, gleys, and anaerobics find a living?

Social planners have, of late years, come to use the Sand Counties for a different, albeit somewhat parallel purpose. The sandy region serves as a pale blank area, of pleasing shape and size, on those polka-dot maps where each dot represents ten bathtubs, or five women's auxiliaries, or one mile of black-top, or a share in a blooded bull. Such maps would become monotonous if stippled uniformly.

In short, the Sand Counties are poor.

Perhaps the farmers who did not want to move out of the Sand Counties had some deep reason, rooted far back in history, for preferring to stay. I am reminded of this every April when the pasque-flowers bloom on every gravelly ridge. Pasques do not say much, but I infer that their preference harks back to the glacier that put the gravel there. Only gravel ridges are poor enough to offer pasques full elbow-room in April sun. They endure snows, sleets, and bitter winds for the privilege of blooming alone.

In the 1840's a new animal, the settler, intervened in the prairie battle. He didn't mean to, he just ploughed enough fields to deprive the prairie of its immemorial ally: fire. Seedling oaks forthwith romped over the grasslands in legions, and what had been the prairie region, became a region of woodlot farms.

No important change in ethics was ever accomplished without an internal change in our intellectual emphasis, loyalties, affections, and convictions. The proof that conservation has not yet touched these foundations of conduct lies in the fact that philosophy and religion have not yet heard of it. In our attempt to make conservation easy, we have made it trivial.

Our ability to perceive quality in nature begins, as in art, with the pretty. It expands through successive stages of the beautiful to values as yet uncaptured by language.

Acknowledgments

I am particularly grateful to Frank Terbilcox, the man who singlehandedly implements all of the land management policies at the Leopold Reserve. I never had a question about the place he could not answer or a request he did not grant. His knowledge and energy have left a lasting impression. I also wish to thank my beleaguered inlaws, Fred and Sally Moskol of Madison, Wisconsin, for once again providing me with food, shelter, and companionship at unbeatable rates. And finally, I must acknowledge and congratulate the determination of three personal opponents whose presence on the Leopold Reserve built character in the face of suffering: the mosquitoes of July, the pollen of August, and the North Wind of winter. —*C.S.*

Notes on the photographer and the essayist

Charles Steinhacker is one of the most prolific photographers working today in the fields of natural history and the environment. Books to which he was the sole or principal photographic contributor include *Superior* and *Yellowstone,* and his work has appeared also in *National Geographic* and *Audubon,* among other periodicals. Steinhacker lives in Higganum, Conn., with his wife, Barbara, and a daughter, Kate.

Susan Flader is assistant professor of western and environmental history at the University of Missouri. She is the author of *Aldo Leopold and the Evolution of an Ecological Attitude,* to be published by the University of Wisconsin Press, and is at work on a full biography of Leopold as well. Ms. Flader is a native of Wisconsin and a graduate of its university at Madison, not far from the sand counties.